#Winning against a state employee . . .

- PREFACE-

Child of such purity ...OFSUCH HOPE ...
Innocent ... Precious pure soul...
W ARM . S AFE. @ HOME AND NOTATRISK.

Child of such purity ...
Raised right...
AN ABUNDANCE OF ALL THAT IS LOVING, CARING AND
NURTURING IS EVIDENT BY HOW WELL BOTH GIRLS WERE BEING
RAISED.

CHILD IS LATER VISITING A FAMILY MEMBER N EVER RETURN
FOR SOME GOOD PARENTS. STATE EMPLOYEE CITES,
"Child is safe."

1

#Winning against a state employee . . .

State employee lied. A box of evidence show the complete anti-thesis. Child simply has vanished...

#Winning against a state employee . . .

#WINNING...

(against a state employee …)

AUTHOR:

WOMEN 4 JUSTICE...

IN ASSOCIATION WITH...

T.A.N.

Chapter 1-

Lawyer to represent.

So many had inform me I was not able to sue or my daughter. I remember 1x sitting with a table long of suit wearing lawyer(s) in NJ-DE-PA tri-state down toward South Jersey(right at the border of side of Delaware.) Attorney looked me in the eyes and told me,"Why you don't represent yourself?" You're quite astute in building the mental visual/the mental picture insofar as:

1. Who did what.
2. Who violated you.
3. Who was the mastermind behind such.

4. Able to prove such causal-link.
5. Able to discern per cause of action liability at state AND federal level.
6. Who withheld and such motive that would make a caseworker, state employee engage in such clear act(s) of misconduct that has yes harmed you severely and your daughter's. I looked at him, and said, "Because I want a lawyer."

Even if I am yes fully capable of going pro-se, but I would like an attorney on our team. The firm again conceded to such fact that:

A.) We, the family are yes able to win $$$ damages and how the damage(s)done to us by such DCPP, DYFS DCF employee, their unlawful act(s) are the proximate cause of

5

such injury per year the girls were out of my
primary loving care.We,the injured family
are entitle to highest amount, same as others
who coast-to-coast and in our tri-state are
suffered by policies, procedural being
ignored willfully and knowing by DYFS.

B.) We, the family are suffering and this will be
heard and seen (at trial)if not reasonably
settled by such jury of our peers.

The firm said all of this and then some.

But at the end of the day when it really
mattered? He said, but, I can't represent you.
Our family never gave up. It was clear as day
that many firms like his was full of you know
what.

We did not let such uncaring, non-astute and indolent law firm(s)who want the more simplified lawsuit(s) i.e., car accident, we did **not** let such worthless ostensible lawyer from the old school deter us from executing such suit that we already knew can be won and we continued tirelessly non-stop seven days a week emailing, calling on lawyers worldwide, while learning unremittingly, howw to sue the right way(pro-se)child protection services, by deadlinc and bcgan doing just that.

CHAPTER 2

"Someone...Somewhere...

doesn't want you to have your kids."

When I parked, to go inside and meet another lawyer in northern part of NJ outside of(15 min.,from Times Square in Manhattan(NYC) such firm consist of black lawyers/Hispanic(Dominican)

I recall this meeting quite well as these lawyers greeted me and assume I was at first "joking" on what happen.

Such information I've discovered/factual and all withheld is not something that is found usually by a parent, or so I have been told by this firm who again did not believe me,

 until I provided such lawyer phone number who had boxes of the same proof(s)I had to support:

- ➢ Fraud on the court by a state employee.
- ➢ Knowingly. Willfully disregard court orders.
- ➢ Malice.
- ➢ A conspired act.
- ➢ Withheld information that was to establish how a state employee hid a child suffering at a home, where it was prevalent knowledge to be a drug-infested/alcoholic household and proof that the state employee lied for not a day a month… but years on end as long as

it meant child was to remain no matter how unlawful, with a troubled set of adults.

> Proof foster strangers had my daughters, at least one of them. As a result of such foster care 1 of my girls were ignored, mistreated maltreatment was clear and severe harm for a long time.
> The other child, my youngest was being threaten by her own step-mom that if she "keep it up she is going to foster care next."
>
> Such evidence to the firm I was sitting with blew each attorney away, and each male lawyer and 1 hispanic/Dominican (woman) had all reviewed looking quite befuddled at how a state agency DCPP worker can do this

to a good loving ciizen and mom in our state said," *__We want__* your case." Sign here…. I said, thank you. Lawyer(s)cited, "You're going to win for each day you were lied upon…

➢ Falsely accused.
➢ Slandered/Defamed by such incompetent, jealous, hateful worthless good for nothing state employees at Division Youth Family Services, aka DCPP, DCF.
➢ For each day you cried each day and night for such girls, for each minute you did not get to:
➢ Hug your daughters as you did for first 10 yrs and 7 yrs., of their very young lives.
➢ Tuck them in at night once legally kidnap.
➢ Each day you're force to hear DYFS, DCF lies on how they were doing, then learning

such SHOCK the girls's were suffering without you for a long time.
SIGN HERE...

I was thrilled. I began to sign such contract as it cites the typical (In my state) is 33 and a third percent of whatever is won with such law firm. I was a happy woman again. I seen hope again. It was not until later when I got home and I recall being able to relax. I took a hot bath and read a book I was working on as I focus on legal studies. Then... I was able to fall asleep without feeling so depressed that I would not be

able to procure lawyer and I was asleep first time, in a long time a full 8 to nine hours. Phone rings next morning. Lawyer(s)said,

"We can't represent you." I ask why not.

 What has changed within 24hours? Lawyer cite that "someone …somewhere doesn't want you to have your girls anymore.(A lead attorney said this at the firm.)I knew what the firm meant. I did not falter nor attempt to implore a firm to stay on with me, through this long haul, the fight for such FINAL justice against CPS. I simply said fine. I will win on my own such justice I and my daughter deserve. I hung up. But before I concluded such call the lead counsel at the firm says, "Another firm though might still represent your injured family." You have enough also to win this all pro-se.

Chapter 3

The Moment.

I remember such lawyer and him saying what he said, shared in previous chapter. I recall that morning taking a drive, after such let-down by such cowardly weak non-astute uncaring firm, and I turned on my music in the car. I went and sat alone in a nearby beach that I love, and I simply sat on a bench with my thoughts and strategy-book insofar as if I was really ready to do all this on my own. **I was ready.**

God showed me such correct trajectory to follow.

I knew I would have to stand TALL and stay STRONG and get down to business. I knew at "that moment."

I would not only sue C.P.S. (Division Youth and Family Services #dyfs #dcf #dcpp)but I will do such an astounding job & ergo, on my own, be able to win. So many online, I told a close friend, over mi casa(my house) having dinner, have not sued a cps worker. The reasons are simple (no lawycr.)I did not want to be this way, and I am not a quitter so I made sure after dinner I would execute such meritorious suit against a worker who lied and falsified, and as a result my child suffered. BAD.

My close friend said,

#Winning against a state employee . . .

"If anyone, while pro-se can win against a no good, incompetent agency and or its individual workers at the DCPP dyfs that is you, Mamita.

I smiled.

Walked my company out after dinner. Booted up computer. Got the law books out and I began. **No looking back**. **My mission** was not in any way unclear.

Rob a child of his or her good parent…of her or his grandparent..of their childhood-innocence?

Expect to *pay for it* ***in a court of law*** *when finally,*

Child Protection Services is now a **DEFENDANT.**

Children **deserve** as good parents, <u>FINAL</u> justice..

when deprived intentionally by DCFS…

17

<u>Chapter 4</u>

"As I prepare this morning to sue today DCF the world has changed within the many years of my

living in sorrow & agony…

We have had the first Black president with his tall **lovely strong independent astute loyal** wife, his bff first lady Michelle, and the love both share is a love any astute man and woman want and will **never** settle for less. *#I_love_their_love premise on being real.* Not a **superficial** love, but **mutual respect**/honor. Not **dis-honor.**

Yes. The world we live in has really altered so much.

But, what has not changed though is the overflowing love for my daughter's who were as even attorneys agree, "legally kidnapped" and I realize no matter how much since the day of removal years prior,

I had to get them back.

But meanwhile I had to start to execute such lawsuit and I will share with you all how I did it, on my own, to see my multi-million lawsuit$ for state/federal damages,

how I was able to properly astutely and justly allow for such magistrate(in federal

19

court) to agree with me, so that my lawsuit was able to survive what is known everyone when suing a state employee a M.T.D.(as read in other books we have published…)

The motion to dismiss leading to *summary judgement.*

Chapter 5

CAUSE OF ACTION AGAINST CPS(CHILD PROTECTION SERVICES PURSUANT TO SECTION 1983 85 and 86

#Winning against a state employee . . .

When you're suing a cps/and or any state employee such cause of action has to be unclear, right to the point and conforming to such rules of the court that you're attempting to file. I did not file in state court. I had made a conscious decision to go ahead to the United States District Court.(Federal) I have not 1 regret doing so either.

Early on…

I wanted the federal court to know it all. Not leaving one stone un-turned. Then I was learning as a pro-se self file litigant suing a state employee that you do not have to write a book but a brief narrative insofar as what has transpired with other brief relevance to one's viable claim to get started.

#Winning against a state employee . . .

The first time I worked on my suit to attempt to perfect it, I was not sure what I was doing. Then, in no time I had mastered such craft of artfully drafting it to such perfection.

We didn't know much about the law, how it works in our favor as much as we know now.

We share our story with you, on paperback, in hopes such winning lawsuit filed by way of pro-se method will help another.

If our book(s)help one innocent good family, then our job is done, praise God as we never want you all to go through what we have.

The second statutory prong requires the Division to show a parent is unable or unwilling to eliminate the harm facing the child. N.J.S.A. 30:4C 15.1(a)(2). The focus of this inquiry is to determine "whether the parent has cured and overcome the initial harm that endangered the health, safety, or welfare of the child, and is able to continue a parental relationship without recurrent harm to the child." K.H.O., supra, 161 N.J. at 348. Alternatively, the State may show "that the parent is unable to provide a safe and stable home for the child and that the delay in securing permanency continues or adds to the child's harm." Id. at 348 49.

 The withdrawal of nurture and care for an extended period of time is itself a harm that endangers the health and development of the child. D.M.H., supra, 161 N.J. at 379. "

The question is whether the parent can become fit in time to meet the needs of the child." N.J. Div. of

Youth & Family Servs. v. T.S., 417 N.J. Super. 228, 244 (App. Div. 2010), certif. denied, 205 N.J. 519 (2011).

See also N.J. Divcertif. denied, 180 N.J. 456 (2004)

What you're reading on prior page,and above section of this book, DYFS failed,at each level to assist the parent in reunifying, by law, and to cure the reason insofar as why the child was taken in the first place. Such child and her little sister lost almost 8 years at home with mom.

#Winning against a state employee . . .

"Family of author is **additionally** asking for punitive."

P unitive damages may be awarded where the plaintiff proves "that the harm suffered was the result of the defendant's acts or omissions, and such acts or omissions were actuated by actual malice or accompanied by a wanton and willful disregard of persons who foreseeably might be harmed by those acts or omissions." **N.J.S.A. §2A:15-5.12.**

Such public entity is liable for injury proximately caused by an act or omission of an employee, within the scope of her or his employment, IF the act or such omission, would, apart from this section, have given rise to such cause of action against that employee and or his representative.
-
Generally as our author studies teach,

that an employee of a public entity i.e, DYFS (DCPP,DCF et.al,) is LIABLE for his torts to the same extent, as a private person, and moreover, the public entity is "vicariously liable" for ANY injury which its employee causes, to the "same extent" as a private employer.

See Societa per Azioni De Navigazione Italia v. City of L.A.,Cal. 3d 446, 463 (Cal.1982)

Be sure everyone to study hard,and realize that
when suing such public employee,
 i.e,

DCF child protection services worker,who was
prior assigned to your case,and or currently and has
cause such grave harm, to you and your family,
besides suing while you're pro-se, statutory claim(s)
there are also such common law claims i.e., but not
limited to claim for the defendant, for which you're
suing,as our founder has correctly done i.e, for
intentional tort; ***interference*** with one's right to
upbringing(raising one's child et.al, & the
freedoms,liberties, deprivation of one's right(14th
Amendment) ***the intentional infliction*** of emotional

distress defamation(slander) libel,to malicious prosecution.

However,make sure you're placing the defendants at CPS on proper notice(and timely) as case law support, strict requirement(s)exist prior to the institution of your lawsuit for **damages.**
See: VELEZ v. City of Jersey City, 358 NJ Super,224,239-240 (APP.DIV.) 2003;and or Bonitis v. New Jersey Inst.of Tech (2003) where it is clear that the failure to first place the entity,

and or the individual that you are suing for such damages, associated with such injury violation et.al, shall be barred under **NJ TORT ACT**, for such failure to meet the notice of tort claim requirements of the ACT against the individual employee(s) charged with an intentional tort, as well as everyone the public entity.

Chapter 6

Parental Rights v. CPS

Such parenting rights for which naturally a biological parent has such inherent right, liberty as case law wholly support per state, in the actual raising, nurturing, interest in simply parenting such child.

Such right,and one's liberty <mark>interest</mark> supercedes the bumbling of the agency employees @ Child Protection Services, so make a note of that everyone. When you're astute,and or becoming more astute, prudently sentient,(aware) you're going to do just fine when suing **BY DEADLINE** pro-se self file abhorrent caseworker, social workers, et.al, at:

#Winning against a state employee . . .

#DCF,#DHR, #DCFS,#DYFS #DCPP, #ACS,
#CHFS #DFS #DHHS #DSHS #DCYF #DFPS
#CHIPS #ACS #DSS child protection service
employees nationwide.

E-Help form, click to begin your POWER session
1-on-1 to begin same day.(See main site and call in)
during hours of operation.

Chapter 7

Knowingly…Willfully….

Our research at our advocate-student learning ctr.,
we learned how a woman(former DCF
employee)sued and revealed so much in her
deposition/lawsuit et.al, and won in the end.
She has revealed things that the author already
knew. The level such agency employee(s)will go to
is befuddling, it makes you wonder how can a
male/female state employee sleep at night after
doing such, involving the innocent and most of all,
an innocent child, and family. A former (employee)
had sued DYFS,DCPP for a cover up, where
(a supervisor) at the cps nj agency attempt to conceal
such actual facts of the actual case involving a
parent. Such hand-written"case note from a dyfs
supervisor, happen to **disappear** that firmly support this
DCF NJ claim says the plaintiff.

However, as the suit cites, it still demonstrates the supervisor's attempt to cover-up ***and to conceal*** his own negligent acts/negligence so that (involving the family, the mother case)such negligent acts would ultimately be blame later, "on the actual assigned caseworker." **She won Quarter of a million in damages.**

Her suit that has been won had cited things in there our author and others are acclimated with and it was pretty much mind-blowing to see just how a 'supervisor' would treat his own caseworker, in which this woman Tracy Barco turned around and sue and she won against the agency. i.e,
At a meeting in Mercer County(NJ) the photos involving a child abuse victim, was shown. Such supervisor who is being sued by his caseworker, who won, had admitted that she as others was told do not leave "a child" in nj who is at "risk."

The supervisor says the plaintiff(Barco) said how he's *responsible* for the child abuse **the child, did suffer**, yet a dyfs, dcpp, dcf supervisor was **trying** to make it look as if it was her own fault,and was his. Again this is featured in winning suit under Tracy Barco,former dcf employee.

In the author daughter's prior family court case, *a reasonable jury* experts cite will want to know as any parent and family themselves living such nightmare with such fraud on the court by a cps employee:

Where are:
1.)case task per employee along with such closure file(s)detailing per daughter.

2.)Where are the visit and call log(s)checking up on the girls, and proof it was done when ordered, if any.

3.)Where are the pink conference notes that would have directed case task etc., and closure.
-

The extreme efforts of a supervisor, as in the author's lawsuit, carlos novoa and or also another supervisor by the name of Migdalia Diaz, attempted to cover it all up and or Sebastian Antony, as others, is clear and **based _on a preponderance_** of the evidence, with a jury hearing these set of facts,
can be proven and result is damages jury trial **IF** not reasonably settled." Such incident(s) clearly demonstrate flagrant attempt to put the blame on DYFS caseworker, rather than the actual one's in charge, supervisor NOVOA and or Diaz, Antony to prevent him, and or the female supervisor, from being held responsible,if sued, for such case practice, dyfs negligence leading to a media story/coverage, and or a lawsuit.

Such blatant attempts for so many years to conceal, _**by a state employee is quite ubiquitous.**_

**Nationwide…**

The only difference is the owner of T.A.N. & Women4JusticePublishing NYC was able to ***prove*** the abhorrent and unlawful act(s)as the concealment, perjury to a material fact, and has awaited her day in court, to finally share with a jury for damages.

Such concealment, only further demonstrates such attempt by the defendant's being sued to cover up and continually at each turn, to conceal his/her own negligent act(s) to see to it a loving good parent was deprived her right to continue to nurture, love care for her daughter's.

Case practice negligence is clear in the author lawsuit.

In a suit filed by a caseworker...(BARCO) who did win against the troublesome agency(BARCO) clearly cites,

"how such workers at NJ Child Protection Services worker would be blame when a child is hurt/in danger and or left in harm's way, and how some cases are close even prior to seeing the child at risk, and how the supervisor's would place blame with such,and on the assigned caseworker, in order to prevent the assigned supervisor from being held liable for damages, case practice, and other related negligence."

Chapter 8

Living Proof of CPS unlawful act(s)by a state employee and winning (***in the end***)

When such unlawful tactic(s)by a social worker at DCF that were utilized as a means to harm such loving children and innocent good parent, it doesn't go away as it is 10x worse to learn in a withheld file internal caseworker notes, and other evidence, that it was done with such intent. Author is living proof however, you're able to transcend and overcome when suing timely per civil right damages pursuant to Section 83 and win.

Chapter 9

DCFS **non**-compliance is prevalent.

State employee @ CPS and their continual inability to comply, to such rules, regulations, adhere to such policies seemingly applies to so many social workers whether in the NYC,Massachusetts, Iowa, Kentucky, Maryland, NJ/DE tri-state, MD.,NC, PA., Arizona to California and all states in between and yet, a caseworker always want the parent or grandparent and others to comply,and or if not you're threaten by the worker to have your rights terminated.

Good more are suing premise on such fact…

When CPS has failed to properly intervene,

a **child is 10x more at risk,**

per removal statistics reveal nationwide.

Such child dying, or becoming a rape victim under state dcfs supervision when the little girl, teen-child can be home is completely **inexcusable**.

Caseworkers in CALIFORNIA to NYC-DE-NJ has had multiple instances, so many opportunities to **effectively and timely intervene, but chose not to.**

As a result?

A child is raped, or sexually abused,molested, psychological-emotional traumatization, breakdown, and or have gone missing, placed on drugs under state supervision, when the child should have by law, been home. Good luck hence suing CPS (the right way properly and correctly.)If the owner,of our effective astute caring 1 of a kind ctr.,

was able to do so (prior to applying at law schools, then there is no reason why you can't.

<u>DEADLINE</u> however does exist and will arrive before you know it, so #focus and do not become un-focus....1-929-277-7848.

Lawsuit against North Carolina, Indiana,Arizona,Pennsylvania,Texas California,Louisiana,DE.,NJ,Chicago,Georgia, Alaska,Hawaii, Montana,New Hampshire,Westchester County, NY, The Bronx, Manhattan, Connecticut,Oregon,Michigan,

#Winning against a state employee . . .

Maryland, WASHINGTON and nationwide against DCS are growing.

<u>Best</u> part about it?

So many who are luckily to still able to execute such warranted suit (the <u>right way</u> and correctly)are learning per day,per session, that you always had it inside of you,but just needed support at educational and encouragement/empowerment level
#teamwork

Those who just "talk about it" not apply strategic action, shall continue to <u>FALTER</u>."

Chapter 10

CHILD PROTECTION EMPLOYEES.

Caseworkers, social workers CPS over-reach, and shall continue to lie under oath/perjury to a material fact, and have done so as studies show, one too many times removing one's happy healthy child from their loving home, *without a legal basis,* as seen in the founder own winning suit pro-se self file moving forward(approve to move forward by recent adjudication by U.S.District FEDERAL court 3rd cir;)into the private, and the sacred, constitutionally sacrosant area of such family and hence infringes upon the liberties, the interest of the parent.

Chapter 11

Visit link about a lawsuit won for $800,000 against DCFS/County who violated a mother parental rights and the children rights of such woman who was

#Winning against a state employee . . .

innocenthttp://suecps.weebly.com/almost-one-million-dollars-won-involving-a-loving-parent-whose-child-was-removed-without-a-court-order-or-a-warrant-for-removal-1-929-277-7848-ext-806.html

Update(s)in our books and on our popular websites,
 for those who were not aware that
 another parent in CALIFORNIA,had sued multiple
child protection services workers, know as in CALI
#DCFS and also encompassed in her family suit was the
other defendant, the County.

Such parent, once again had sued and won civil right
damage(s)associated with removal of her children."
Almost One Million Dollars...

 Multiple social workers for the DCFS agency reportedly
in such lawsuit had falsified a report,and or fabricated
such statement(s) relating to the children,
 by making it appear parent injured child.

43

 Never happened.

Congratulations Mirtha Lopez...

#FIGHT 4 WHAT IS RIGHT or keep being treated by dcfs the way no good human deserve. It is all up to you our many readers. 1-929-277-7848 Ext 1359 . . . Good luck against CPS when you are suing by deadline for per damages associated with a cps violation. #**be proud** and take back your rights while doing so."

Help form…(featured on main site …)

T.A.N. is a nation's first, **1-on-1** network for those suing just like the owner has astutely and timely have done for damages associated with a state employee(s) malfeasance and all injuries pursuant to: Section 1983, 85,86 under:

#Winning against a state employee . . .

Title 42 involving one's *federally-protected* right…

Chapter 12

Child is at no risk, your honor

When the author learned, as media validate, learned her daughter's were (**not** where the state agency employee(s)said they were in approximately forty-one subsequent family court hearings,

as news/media validate & how the girls were both **"thriving/doing well/no risk"** but she knew the truth will arise by never giving up + **would** hold all accountable as her family once the evidence supporting what she inwardly knew has arised."

Such evidence as experts local/state & nationwide has all agreed, is "more than what is usually warranted to win her damages as her daughter's once it makes it to the proper court along with the actual ongoing "federal violation" not hard to prove based on the preponderance of the evidence against employees over @ #DCF #DCPP #CPS who for almost a decade lied, **falsified**, altered,

withheld evidence for quite some time when such suburban good mom and woman and her daughter's lives were filled with what ALL Good American loving families and worldwide would want in their everyday lives...

#Winning against a state employee . . .

Author's family have WON such relevant right(approve by magistrate) to have their $50MILLION DOLLARS civil right/constitutional rights, gross-negligence, lawsuit to move forward against DCF employees. She launch during such time the nation's very 1st **EFFECTIVE** learning on *1-on-1 educational empowerment interactive online motivational and daily consulting biz org.of its kind.*

While she continue to one day push toward the implementation of a JURIS DOCTOR(law degree)she shall continue to demonstrate such agressiveness, focus & demonstrate the overall erudition, insofar as the proper pro-se navigation throughout her own meritorius lawsuit filed just in time, by deadline **when at first(118+lawyers) that author was not able** to sue a state employee…

#Winning against a state employee . . .

Our boss at T.A.N. knew better than such fallacy, hence has effectively sued CPS all while acting pro-se (self file)without a lawyer and now continue to be lauded by lawyers worldwide on doing so at the level most have not..." The author @ Ext.806 was able to pierce the immunities when she timely by DEADLINE facilitated in a timely manner and filed her meritorious lawsuit for various violations and the ongoing continual federal civil right, constitutional rights violation et.al., against multi-social workers,caseworkers assigned to her daughter's prior farce of a "removal case by CPS, DCF employees, DYFS,now known as DCPP. There was no time to sleep. Author continually and aggressively studied the law.Darkness under her once sparklie happy joyful sultry eyes became more dim, yet her sad and painful stressful-tired eyes had proved her never-ending determination seven days week to learn as much as was humanly able,

to study law and make sure <u>all</u> would be held lawfully accountable. Her studies went deep into the night.

(**Sleep**) she once told a news reporter, covering her warranted suit, can come later *AFTER FINAL JUSTICE* is visible …

Media has validated such relevance of her lawsuit pro-se,proving ALL ostensible and indolent lawyers of the "old school wrong." E-form must be properly implemented to call the same day to begin your 1-on-1 POWER educational learning session."1-929-277-7848 Ext.920

Now, for those nationwide who are not acclimated with the workings of the U.S.Constitution Equal Protection Clause, in relevant part, i.e.,(in example) (a cps child protection employee are not allowed to violate one's rights simply because you're not approving of them, and or do not like such person or are an outright racist/and or discriminating against such loving parent for other reasons. When it comes to the ***unlawful*** conduct of a #DCFS CPS employee more times than not, as our research wholly support.

Chapter 13-

CPS rely on a **#*False*Allegation** each and every time without an iota of truth …

Multiple state cps employees only have an anonymous allegation(s)for which is to the more reasonable average prudent mind just that, an allegation, no actual evidence of such serious harm, hence, as case law per state support, **is not** enough to deny and unconstitutionally deprive a loving parent, such natural biological parent their own child." Owner, of T.A.N. and

#Winning against a state employee . . .

Women4Justice Publishing N.Y.C., would keep notes as you all should be doing, and would facilitate each phase of her winning civil rights lawsuit through and through without a burn-out. **No time** to slow down.

She kept a note _**of each**_ call/message/words verbatim said by a **lying** caseworker soon to be sued for damage(s) and buried her little nose in law book(s)not just local law,state **but FEDERAL** nationwide **per state** and has mastered such craft that has been clearly demonstrative insofar her pro-se suit against cps.

Chapter 14

How we loved…the 1st snowfall …

Winter….the author's favorite season and her girls, each winter late November/December through end of March, always looked forward to winter.."

#Winning against a state employee . . .

The snow is always most beautiful when it falls and lingers-on the trees, glistening.

Winter never appeared the same without authors little beauties @ home.

So much time a family of such good lost.

At *no fault* of their own …DFS DCPP state employee will be sued she would tell those close to her,and not just sued…But sued RIGHT, and without no mistakes after what has happened to her life, her daughter's and such pro-se #winning suit shall help many others still S.I.T.S. (stuck in the system)and injured **VIOLATED** by a state worker.

#JUSTICEisFinallyNear

Chapter 15

"DCPP **don't** care what the law says <u>until</u> a state employee is served with a lawsuit, experts agree.."

The state of New Jersey, as case law wholly support requires the Division to show a parent is unable or unwilling to eliminate *the harm facing the child. N.J.S.A. 30:4C 15.1(a)(2).*

The focus is to determine "whether the parent has cured **and overcome** the **initial** harm that endangered the health, safety, or welfare of the child, and is able to continue a parental relationship without recurrent harm to the child." K.H.O., supra, 161 N.J. at 348. Alternatively, the State may show

55

"that the parent is unable to provide a safe and stable home for the child and **that the delay in securing permanency continues or adds to the child's harm**." Id. at 348 49.

The *withdrawal* of nurture and care for an ***extended period*** of time is itself a ***harm*** that endangers the health and development of the child. D.M.H., supra, 161 N.J. at 379. "

The question is whether the parent can become fit in time to meet the needs of the child." N.J. Div. of Youth & Family Servs. v. T.S., 417 N.J. Super. 228, 244 (App. Div. 2010), certif. denied, 205 N.J. 519 *(2011)*(reiterating that as public policy increasingly focuses on a child's need for permanency, "the emphasis has shifted from protracted efforts for reunification with a birth parent to an expeditious, permanent placement to promote the child's well-being."

All of the prior page and above was again ignored even after multi-subsequent appeals, by state worker, in violation of the author's family rights. #LEARN #PROTECTYOURSELF so you do not have to go through what the owner went through.

If she knew earlier, what she know now, a suit would have been filed yes, but her girls would've not been detained unlawfully for as long as the 2 were. Hence, the basis as to why we at the TAN network exist, until God calls us home…So you can #learn #fight-right and #Empowered and educated to avoid such a nightmare.(In author's case for thirteen to 14 yrs at time of book publishing.)

In the conclusion of this most warranted book,along with the entire docu-series…Remember that when you are applying such strategic-action and are focus you're able to as the author hold #DCF accountable.

Lawsuits in NJ against DCPP have grown and shall only continue as per other state when you're child has been unlawfully seized/continually detained in violation of one's fourteenth and fourth amendment right.

The law(s)are not in any way unclear.

You are able to learn when suing pro-se such state employee that you're astute enough to do so, even when lawyer says the complete antithesis.So, don't give up.***That's exactly*** what CPS employees want you to do.

#Winning against a state employee . . .

This was of **<u>no option</u>** for the author. If such books, and consulting 1-on-1, if such prowess for years of owner of T.A.N. help even 1 innocent GOOD American and others worldwide,then her job is done. We thank you for reading another part of our series. Look out for other books analogous as her fight for FINAL JUSTICE for her family shall continue…

#Stay Focus …

And never give up.

Help/Hotline/Consulting 1-on-1

1-929-277-7848

#Winning against a state employee . . .

A mother's will to for what is right.

A mother's pain …

A *good* family tears…

Shall *ultimately* become...

Their *FINAL* **Justice**.

#JUSTICE is Finally Near …

Our rights …do matter … EXT. 1359